Derek Jeter

and the NEW YORK YANKEES

2000 WORLD SERIES

by Michael Sandler

Consultant: Jim Sherman
Head Baseball Coach
University of Delaware

BEARPORT
PUBLISHING

New York, New York

Credits

Cover and Title Page, © Ezra O. Shaw/Allsport/Getty Images; 4, © Jeff Haynes/ AFP/Getty Images; 5, © Al Bello/Getty Images; 6, © Anthony Dugal Photography; 7, © Anthony Dugal Photography; 8, © Anthony Dugal Photography; 9, © Diamond Images/Getty Images; 11, © Jamie Squire/Getty Images; 12T, © Jerry Driendl/Getty Images; 12B, © Ambient Images Inc./Alamy; 13, © T.G. Higgins/Getty Images; 14, © John Mabanglo/AFP/Getty Images; 15, © Doug Kanter/AFP/Getty Images; 16, © Reuters/Mike Segar; 17, © REUTERS/Ray Stubblebine; 18, © Stan Honda/AFP/Getty Images; 19, © Al Tielemans/Sports Illustrated; 20, © AP Images/Matt Campbell; 21, © Jed Jacobsohn/ALLSPORT/Getty Images; 22T, © Vincent Laforet/Allsport/Getty Images; 22C, © REUTERS/Mike Blake; 22B, © Vincent Laforet/Allsport/Getty Images.

Publisher: Kenn Goin
Senior Editor: Lisa Wiseman
Creative Director: Spencer Brinker
Design: Stacey May
Photo Researcher: Omni-Photo Communications, Inc.

Library of Congress Cataloging-in-Publication Data

Sandler, Michael.
 Derek Jeter and the New York Yankees : 2000 World Series / by Michael Sandler.
    p. cm. — (World series superstars)
 Includes bibliographical references and index.
 ISBN-13: 978-1-59716-641-6 (library binding)
 ISBN-10: 1-59716-641-3 (library binding)
 1. Jeter, Derek, 1974- 2. Baseball players—United States—Biography—Juvenile literature. 3. New York Yankees (Baseball team) —Juvenile literature. 4. World Series (Baseball) (2000) —Juvenile literature. I. Title.

 GV865.J48S32 2008
 796.357092—dc22
 (B)
                          2007031361

For more information, write to Bearport Publishing Company, Inc., 101 Fifth Avenue, Suite 6R, New York, New York 10003. Printed in the United States of America.

10 9 8 7 6 5 4 3 2 1

 Contents

Subway Series

For the first time in 44 years, there was a **Subway Series** in New York. Who would win the 2000 World Series—the Yankees or the Mets?

Game 4 was **critical** for the Yankees. A Mets win would tie the series.

One lifelong Yankees fan wasn't going to let that happen. That fan was Yankees **shortstop** Derek Jeter.

Derek Jeter

Yankees pitcher Orlando Hernandez signs autographs before the start of the Subway Series.

From the time he was eight years old, Derek wanted to play baseball for the New York Yankees.

A Young Yankees Fan

As a child, Derek spent each summer visiting his grandparents in New Jersey. They lived close to New York City.

During those trips, Derek became a big Yankees fan. He watched them play on TV. He listened to games on the radio. Sometimes, his grandma even took him to Yankee Stadium.

Back home in Michigan, Derek told his friends that he'd play for New York one day. They laughed. Skinny kids from Michigan don't grow up to play for the Yankees!

Derek and his family

Derek grew up in
Kalamazoo, Michigan.

Derek shares a birthday with
Abner Doubleday, the man
some claim invented the
game of baseball.

Perfect Pick

For Derek, however, his dream was not a laughing matter. He worked hard on his **fielding**. He spent hours practicing his swing. He pumped weights to build up his skinny arms.

By high school, Derek was a strong, talented shortstop. **Scouts** from the **major leagues** came from all over to watch him play.

In 1992, Derek was chosen in Major League Baseball's **amateur draft**. Which team picked him? The New York Yankees!

Derek was on the Kalamazoo Central High School baseball team.

Derek fielding a ball shortly after being drafted by the Yankees.

Only five players were picked ahead of Derek in the whole draft.

Making It Big

Derek was thrilled to be a Yankee! For a few years, he played in the **minor leagues**. Then, in 1996, he made it to their major-league club.

He impressed his teammates from the start. Derek knocked out **clutch hits** and was strong in the field.

After the season ended, Derek was named **Rookie** of the Year. However, he was even prouder of something else. He helped the Yankees win their first World Series in 18 years.

Derek's rookie baseball card

NEW YORK YANKEES™

1ST ROUND DRAFT PICK

DEREK JETER .... PINNACLE

The Yankees celebrate
a World Series win.

Along with stars such as
Bernie Williams and Mariano
Rivera, Derek led the Yankees
to **titles** in 1998 and 1999.

Crosstown Rivals

The only people not impressed with Derek were Mets fans. Fans of the New York teams were fierce **rivals**.

As Derek, Bernie, and Mariano helped the Yankees win title after title, Mets fans watched jealously. The Mets had had some great moments, too. They won the World Series in 1969 and 1986. For the most part, though, they played in the shadow of their **Bronx** neighbors.

The Mets play at Shea Stadium (top) in Queens, New York. It's about 8 miles (13 km) away from Yankee Stadium (bottom) in the Bronx.

Mookie Wilson helped the Mets beat the Boston Red Sox in the 1986 World Series.

Before the 2000 season, the Mets had only two World Series wins. The Yankees had 25!

The Mets Make It

In 2000, the Mets won 94 games. They roared through the **playoffs**. They entered the World Series as **National League** champions.

Who would they face? Derek and the Yankees! For the third straight year, the Yankees took the **American League** crown. Derek couldn't wait. Though he'd been in three World Series already, this one was different. "We're playing the Mets," he said. "It's going to be special."

Derek reaches for a ground ball during the 2000 playoffs.

The Mets enjoy a win during the 2000 playoffs.

In the World Series, the National League champion plays the American League champion in a best-of-seven series. The first team to win four games takes the title.

Bring It On

The Subway Series began on October 21, 2000, at Yankee Stadium. The Yankees won the first two games. Derek played well. In Game 2, he even scored the winning run.

The Yanks seemed unbeatable. Now they had won 14 straight World Series games.

The Mets, though, weren't giving up. The series moved over to Shea Stadium. Playing at home gave them a spark. In Game 3, they came from behind to win.

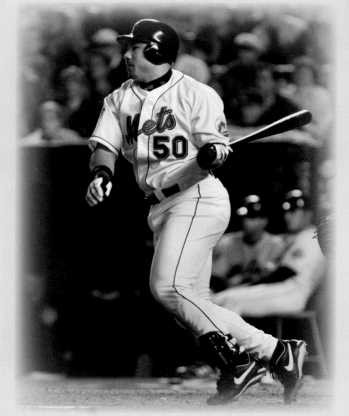

Benny Agbayani hits a game winning double for the Mets in Game 3.

Though the Yankees lost Game 3, Derek still played his best.

The first Subway Series was held in 1921. The New York Giants played the Yankees. The Giants won!

Derek Takes Over

To win Game 4, the Yankees needed a strong start. As **lead-off hitter**, it was Derek's job to provide one.

On the very first pitch of the game, he took a mighty swing. The ball soared across the field. Going . . . going . . . gone! It was a home run for Derek.

The Yankees went on to win. With a 3-1 series lead, they were just one game away from the title.

Derek at the plate in the first inning of Game 4

Yankees pitcher
Mariano Rivera helped
his team win Game 4.

Derek's home run was his first
ever in a World Series.

Champions Again

In Game 5, the Mets fought hard to stay alive. Pitcher Al Leiter threw strikeout after strikeout. After five innings, the Mets led by one run.

As usual, Derek played best when it mattered the most. His sixth inning homer tied the game.

Then, in the ninth inning, Derek's teammates finished the job. Jorge Posada and Scott Brosius scored, giving the Yanks a 4-2 win. Derek and the Yankees were the kings of New York!

Derek is congratulated by the third base coach after his sixth inning home run.

The Yankees became the first team in 25 years to win three straight World Series.

Derek was named MVP (Most Valuable Player) of the 2000 World Series.

★ Key Players ★

Derek, along with some other key players, helped the New York Yankees win the 2000 World Series.

Derek Jeter #2

SS

Bats: Right Throws:

Born: 6/26/1974 in Pequanno
New Jersey

Height: 6′3″ (1.9 m)

Weight: 195 pounds (88 kg)

Series Highlights
Hit the lead-off home run in Game 4
the game-tying home run in Game

Tino Martinez #24

First Base

Bats: Left Throws: Right

Born: 12/7/1967 in Tampa, Florida

Height: 6′2″ (1.88 m)

Weight: 230 pounds (104 kg)

Series Highlight
Hit .364 for the series

Mike Stanton #29

Pitcher

Bats: Left Throws: Left

Born: 6/2/1967 in Houston, Texas

Height: 6′1″ (1.85 m)

Weight: 190 pounds (86 kg)

Series Highlights
Won two games; did not give up a hit in
four relief appearances

★ Glossary ★

amateur draft (AM-uh-chur DRAFT) an event in which major-league teams take turns choosing young athletes to play for them

American League (uh-MER-uh-kuhn LEEG) one of the two major professional baseball leagues in the United States

Bronx (BRONGKS) the area of New York City where the New York Yankees play

clutch hits (KLUHCH HITS) hits made during a critical situation

critical (KRIT-uh-kuhl) very important

fielding (FEELD-ing) catching and throwing the ball while the other team is at bat

lead-off hitter (LEED-awf HIT-ur) the player who is first to bat for a team in any inning

major leagues (MAY-jur LEEGZ) the highest level of professional baseball teams in the United States, made up of the American League and the National League

minor leagues (MYE-nur LEEGZ) baseball teams run by the major-league teams that train young players

National League (NASH-uh-nuhl LEEG) one of the two major professional baseball leagues in the United States

playoffs (PLAY-awfss) games held after the regular season to determine who will play in the World Series

rivals (RYE-vuhlz) people or teams who others compete against

rookie (RUK-ee) a player who is in his or her first year with a professional sports team

scouts (SKOUTS) people who work for major-league teams and search for talented young players

shortstop (SHORT-*stop*) the player whose position is between second and third base

Subway Series (SUHB-*way* SIHR-eez) a World Series played between the two New York baseball teams

titles (TYE-tuhlz) championships; in baseball, World Series wins

Bibliography

Baseball Digest

The New York Times

Sports Illustrated

http://sportsillustrated.cnn.com/baseball/mlb/2000/postseason/

Read More

Donovan, Sandy. *Derek Jeter.* Minneapolis, MN: Lerner (2004).

Fischer, David. *The Story of the New York Yankees.* New York: DK Publishing (2003).

January, Brendan. *Derek Jeter: Shortstop Sensation.* New York: Children's Press (2000).

Learn More Online

To learn more about Derek Jeter,
the New York Yankees, and the World Series, visit
www.bearportpublishing.com/WorldSeriesSuperstars

Index